CHILDREN
OF THE
HOLOCAUST

BY EMILY SCHLESINGER

NONFICTION

SADDLEBACK
EDUCATIONAL PUBLISHING
www.sdlback.com

Photo credits: pages 4/5: Frederic Lewis/Archive Photos via Getty Images; page 5: Christopher Furlong/Getty Images News via Getty Images; page 7: Everett Historical/Shutterstock.com; pages 8/9: Everett Historical/Shutterstock.com; pages 14/15: Szymon Kaczmarczyk/Shutterstock.com; page 15: Everett Historical/Shutterstock.com pages 18/19: Keystone/Hulton Archive via Getty Images; page 25: Hulton Archive/Hulton Archive via Getty Images; page 33: Keystone/Hulton Archive via Getty Images; page 35: Richair/Dreamstime.com; pages 42/43: Fred Morley/Hulton Archive via Getty Images; page 45: Fox Photos/Hulton Archives via Getty Images; pages 48/49: Horace Abrahams/Hulton Archive via Getty Images; pages 52/53: Kurt Hutton/Picture Post via Getty Images; pages 56/57: Christopher Furlong/Getty Images News via Getty Images

ISBN: 978-1-68021-755-1
eBook: 978-1-64598-059-9

Printed in Malaysia

24 23 22 21 20 1 2 3 4 5

Table of Contents

Separation

Edith Weingarten ran as fast as she could. Her parents and three brothers did too. All around them, people fled for their lives. Officers yelled at them in German. Then they took aim. Anyone who could not run fast enough was shot. That was when Edith began to lose her family.

In 1941, **Nazis** came to Edith's home. Her family was Jewish. They lived in Czechoslovakia. The officers told her family to pack. They had to board a train to Poland. That would be their new home. Everyone would get houses and businesses there. That's what the Nazis said.

Instead, they got off the train and were told to run. Edith's mother quickly collapsed. As Edith held her, an officer shouted. He told the girl she would be going to work. She had to leave her mother behind. That was the first separation.

THE START OF WORLD WAR II

In the late 1930s, Nazi Germany began invading other countries. First, they took over Austria. Next, they went into Czechoslovakia. Then, in 1939, they invaded Poland. Two days later, Britain and France declared war on Germany. This was the start of World War II.

Those who remained after the run were lined up. Men went in one line. Women went in another. Edith watched her father and three brothers disappear. She was just a teen. Her family was gone.

The Nazis put Edith to work. They took her to a **ghetto**. Her job was to wash diapers. There were 300 babies. Their parents had been sent away.

Later, the babies were put on trucks. The people caring for them were killed. But Edith and her friend Leah crawled into a **cellar**. For a few days, they hid near the furnace. No one found them. When the Nazis left, the girls sneaked out.

This was the first of many escapes. Edith's journey had just begun. Thousands of children like her were taken from their families by the Nazis. Not many survived. A few who did were **smuggled** across borders. Others jumped from trains. Many hid in dangerous places. These children beat incredible odds to live. Their stories survived with them.

JEWISH GHETTOS

After invading other countries, the Nazis marked off sections of cities as "ghettos." They forced Jews to live in these areas. The largest ghetto was in Warsaw. This was the capital city of Poland. Almost half a million Jews lived there.

A Deadly Idea

Six million Jewish people were killed in the **Holocaust**. They had not done anything wrong. These people lost their lives for being Jewish. It was a **genocide**.

The events leading up to this started in Germany. A new political party had come to power. It was the Nazi Party. Adolf Hitler was their leader. He became **chancellor** in 1933.

DEMOCRACY TO DICTATORSHIP

Germany held an election in 1932. Hitler's Nazi Party won 230 seats in the government. The Communists won the second-largest number of seats. Several months later, there was a fire in the main government building. The Nazis blamed the Communists. They used the fire as an excuse to take over the government. This made Germany a one-party dictatorship.

FAST FACT: The official name of the Nazi Party was the National Socialist German Workers' Party.

Germany had lost World War I. That was 15 years earlier. Since then, their economy had suffered. Many Germans did not have jobs. They were angry with their leaders.

Hitler told these Germans a story. He said they were a "master race." This meant they were better than others. They would take over the world. The name he gave them was Aryans. Hitler's story made them feel better about themselves.

Germans had struggled after the war. Hitler said it was not their fault. Instead, he said Jewish people were responsible. Many of them lived in Germany. But Hitler did not accept them as Germans. He began blaming them for every problem. Soon his followers did too.

OTHER VICTIMS

Jewish people were not the only group targeted by the Nazis. People with disabilities were killed. Hundreds of thousands of Roma people were also murdered. These people originally came from northern India. Their language is called Romani. They spread throughout Europe and were known as travelers. In many places, they faced persecution.

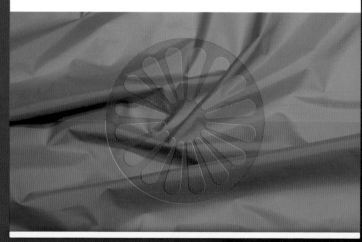

The Nazis passed **anti-Semitic** laws. Jews lost their civil rights. They were not allowed to marry non-Jews. Many children could no longer go to school. Jewish books were burned.

Turning Point

On November 9, 1938, hatred turned to violence. After night fell, a riot began. This had been carefully planned. Hundreds of **synagogues** were burned. Jewish businesses were destroyed. Windows got smashed. Jews were beaten. Police stood by and watched. They did not stop it.

This was Kristallnacht. It means "night of broken glass." Thousands of Jewish men were taken away. Most never returned.

Auschwitz

Edith and Leah had escaped. Still, they were not safe. Poland was under Nazi control.

The girls started walking. They wanted to get back home. But they didn't make it far. Officers found them. Leah was killed. Edith was captured. She was taken to Auschwitz. This was a **concentration camp**.

At the camp, people were lined up. Some were told to go left. They were killed. Edith was sent to the right. She was put to work. Her job was in a factory that made bullets. She worked there for three years.

CONCENTRATION CAMPS

The Nazis first set up concentration camps for what they called "enemies of the state." This included people who spoke out against the Nazi Party. When World War II began, the camps expanded to take in prisoners of war. In 1941, killing centers were set up specifically for the mass murder of Jews. These were also called "death camps."

A Nightmare

Edith could not forget what she saw at the camp.
There were huge rooms. The Nazis said they were
showers. Pipes hung from the ceiling. But these did
not spray water. Instead, they sprayed poison gas.

These were **gas chambers**. Officers led people into
them. They closed the doors. Then the gas was
turned on. Everyone died.

There was a crematorium too. Its fires burned day and night. Bodies went in. Only ashes came out.

Edith heard rumors. People said the Nazis had a goal. They wanted to kill 10,000 Jews per day.

FAST FACT: At Auschwitz, there were 46 ovens in the crematoriums. These could cremate 4,400 bodies each day.

No Place for Children

During the war, thousands of camps were set up. Some were for forced labor. Others were death camps. Auschwitz was the largest of these. Over one million people were killed there.

People arrived at the camps by train. Many were sent to the gas chambers right away. This was because they were not strong enough to work. Older people were in this group. Pregnant women were as well.

Young children were almost always sent to die too. They were little help as workers. The Nazis called them "useless eaters."

FAST FACT: Other large concentration camps were Treblinka and Belzec. More than 750,000 people were killed at Treblinka. Over 600,000 died at Belzec.

Teens might be sent to work. But many of them didn't survive. Conditions were terrible. People starved. Nazis murdered them. Escaping was nearly impossible.

In the death camps, 1.5 million children died. Most were Jewish. A smaller number were Roma.

Young Prisoners

Nazis also kept prisoners of war. Germany had invaded other countries. Poland was one. The Soviet Union was another. Prisoners from these countries were sent to camps. Children were taken from their parents. A few were allowed to live. They had Aryan features. These children were sent to Germany for adoption.

FAST FACT: Blond hair, blue eyes, and fair skin were considered Aryan features.

A TERRIBLE SECRET

There was a secret program. The Nazis started it in 1939. German children with mental and physical disabilities were put to death. Parents of these children were told they were being taken to special clinics. At least 5,000 children were killed in this program.

Lulek

Israel Meir Lau was one of the youngest children to survive a concentration camp. His nickname was Lulek. He was only eight when he was freed. As an adult, Lulek wrote a book about this time. It's called *Out of the Depths.*

Lulek's story started like many others. His family lived in Poland. In 1942, Nazis took away his father and 13-year-old brother. They came for the rest of the family in 1944. A train waited to take them to a camp.

Men formed a line. Lulek's oldest brother, Naphtali, was put in it. He was almost 18. Their mother and Lulek went in another line. This was for women and children. It led to a different car.

They were about to board. Then Lulek's mom had a terrible feeling. She thought they would be killed. As they got near the door, she shoved her son hard. "Take Lulek," she said to Naphtali. He was pushed over to his brother's line. Naphtali smuggled Lulek in.

The train arrived at the camp. Then an officer saw Lulek. He took the brothers to Gestapo headquarters. They were in big trouble. But the officer was willing to take a **bribe**.

Naphtali had no money. He had something else though. His mother had given him a tooth. It had a diamond filling. They gave it to the officer. This bought Lulek's life.

Lulek hid in the barracks. He got food scraps in exchange for polishing shoes.

Another Escape

One day, the camp was attacked. Prisoners were loaded on train cars. Lulek was sent to the car for women and children again.

Naphtali knew his brother would not survive there. The train started moving. At the next stop, Naphtali escaped. He crawled under the train. His body slithered between the rails. Then he climbed up to the next car. "Lulek!" he shouted. There was no answer. Naphtali hurried back.

SECRET POLICE

The Gestapo was the police force set up after Hitler came to power. Some members did not wear uniforms. This made it easy for them to spy on people. They had the authority to arrest anyone for any reason. Many of the tactics they used were brutal.

At each stop, Naphtali tried again. He went to five cars. Finally, Lulek answered. Naphtali used a pin to open the door. The brothers raced back under the belly of the train. They climbed into the men's car. Lulek was safe for now.

Soon they arrived at Buchenwald. This was one of the deadliest camps. Naphtali wrapped Lulek in a pillow. He carried him in a sack on his back.

Then Naphtali saw something happening. Prisoners' bags were being thrown into an oven. He yelled at Lulek to get out of his bag.

NAZI GERMANY

Buchenwald

A German guard spotted the boy. His brother thought fast. Their mom had left him a gold watch. He threw it at the guard. The man let Lulek pass.

A number was assigned to Lulek. It was 117030. Prisoners wore patches too. These were sewn on uniforms. They had shapes and letters. This was how prisoners were **classified**. Lulek's showed he was Jewish. Officers treated Jews the worst.

FAST FACT: Buchenwald did not have gas chambers. Still, many died at the camp. Prisoners starved or got diseases. Others were executed.

117030

Some prisoners liked Lulek. One day, they found a dead body. There was a patch on the man's uniform. It was a red triangle. The letter P was on it. This stood for Polish. They pinned it on Lulek's shirt. Now he had a new identity.

Rumors spread. Officers heard there was a Polish child living with the Jews. They moved Lulek to Block 8. This was for non-Jews. The conditions were much better. That is how Lulek survived until **liberation**.

Prisoner Marking System

The Nazis used numbers, patches, and even tattoos to identify prisoners in concentration camps. Badge colors and shapes had different meanings. All Jews wore a yellow star. Colored triangles could be sewn on top of the star to show other meanings.

BADGE	MEANING
✡	Jewish
▽	Criminal
▽	Political prisoner
▼	Roma
P▽	Polish

6 Life in Hiding

Lulek said his survival took "a chain of miracles." Not many children who went to camps lived. Their best chance was to stay out of the camps in the first place.

Hiding was one way to do this. Many people helped Jewish children hide from the Nazis. Some hid children in attics and ceilings. Others kept them in basements and crawl spaces. These brave people risked their lives. The punishment for hiding Jews was death.

Suse

Suse Grünbaum was Jewish. Her family lived
in Germany. When the Nazis came into power,
they fled. This was when Suse was just two. The
Netherlands was their new home.

Years passed. World War II began. Then Germany
invaded the Netherlands. Suse's family was no
longer safe.

In 1943, they went into hiding. A Dutch family named the Harteminks helped them. They lived on a farm. There was a barn with space under the floor. That is where Suse and her mother hid. Later, the family built them a special hiding place. It was behind a wall. Suse's father was hidden on another farm.

The Harteminks heard there would be a search. Suse and her mother had to be very quiet. Nazis came to the house. Men looked near the hiding place. The wall was hollow. If the officers knocked on it, they would notice. Luckily, they did not knock.

SEARCH AND RISK

Officers did frequent searches. They demanded to enter houses. Then they would look in every corner for signs of life. Neighbors could turn people in. The Nazis offered rewards for any information.

An officer threatened the Harteminks' daughter. He said he knew people were hiding there. If she did not tell the truth, he would shoot her. She denied it. The officer fired a shot. It missed her by just inches. Still, she did not give in.

Next, they went to Mrs. Hartemink. The woman was very religious. They got a Bible and made her swear on it. She did. Finally, the officers left.

Suse and her mother stayed in that hiding place for two years. It was where Suse turned 13. They did not come out until the war ended.

FAST FACT: Experts estimate that only 6 to 11 percent of Jewish children in Europe survived the Holocaust.

Other Hidden Children

Stories like Suse's were common. Many families hid in tiny spaces. This would be hard for anyone. But it was especially hard for children. Officers would come to search. Young children had to be quiet. They did not understand why. Parents gave them treats to keep them from crying.

Sarah Peretz and her mother were living in Poland. She was just three years old. A Catholic policeman warned them that the Nazis were coming. First, he hid them in his home. But that was too risky. Later they moved into a chicken coop. That is where they lived for two years. The little girl was not allowed outside. All she could do was play with the chickens and straw.

FAST FACT: The Nazis invaded Denmark in 1943. With the help of their neighbors, over 90 percent of the country's Jews survived. Most went into hiding and then escaped into Sweden.

Hiding in Plain Sight

There was another way for Jewish children to survive. They could pretend to be from other religions. Some were sent to Christian schools. Catholic **convents** hid others. Muslim families took in children too. The kids could not tell friends who they really were.

Menachem Frankel was one of these children. He was from Belgium. In 1942, his family was sent to a camp. An **underground** group helped him and his sister escape. The two were taken to an **orphanage**. There, Menachem was given a new name. It was Marcel Faure.

Marcel went to church. He celebrated Christian holidays. This was all pretend. But it helped him survive.

A VILLAGE OF HELPERS

One Protestant pastor helped thousands of Jewish children hide. This was in and around the village of Le Chambon-sur-Lignon, France. Jewish children lived in homes, boarding houses, and shelters. The pastor and his helpers created fake identification cards for the refugees.

Living in the Wilderness

Not all children had help. Some were on their own. They hid outdoors.

Charlene Schiff did this. In 1942, her town was going to be destroyed. She escaped with her mother. They hid near a riverbank. Then they heard machine gun fire. For days, they stayed in the water. At one point, Charlene took a nap. When she woke up, her mother was gone.

At just 13, Charlene survived by herself. She hid in the forest. Bugs and tree bark were her meals. It was like that until the end of the war.

Kindertransport

When Hitler came to power, news of his plans spread. Jewish groups all over the world were worried. They feared children were in danger. Some of these groups were in Britain. After Kristallnacht, they spoke with the British government. Together, they made a plan.

Britain set up trains to take children out of Germany. These trains went as far as the North Sea. Then children boarded ships to England. The program was called Kindertransport.

In England, many children were placed with families. Both Jewish and non-Jewish families took them in. Others lived in group homes. The plan was for them to return home when the danger passed.

FAST FACT: The first Kindertransport brought nearly 200 children to Harwich, England. Their orphanage had been burned down on Kristallnacht.

A Difficult Decision

Most children did not understand why they were leaving. Many parents pretended they were going somewhere fun. One girl remembers saying goodbye. Her father tried to joke through his tears. He said she was going on a big adventure. It was the last time she saw him.

Another remembers her grandmother's last words to her. She said there would be "lots of chocolate" where she was going.

Most parents knew they might be saying goodbye forever. It was a painful choice. But it gave their children a chance to survive. Kindertransport saved over 10,000 lives.

A NARROW ESCAPE

Kindertransport only operated for nine months. After war broke out in 1939, the transports stopped. There was one last transport in 1940. German warplanes fired at the ship as it left the port on its way to England.

Kindertransport Routes

Children boarded trains in major cities. These took them to ports in Belgium and the Netherlands. Then ships took them to Harwich, England.

MAP KEY	
————	Train Route 🚂
———	Ship Route 🚢

GREAT BRITAIN

THE NETHERLANDS

BELGIUM

Harwich

Port cities

GERMANY

Berlin

Prague

POLAND

CZECHOSLOVAKIA

Vienna

FRANCE

AUSTRIA

The End of the War

In April 1945, **Allied** troops pushed into Germany. They made it to Berlin. This was the capital. Hitler was cornered. He did not want to face capture. Instead, he killed himself. Germany surrendered. World War II ended soon after. Those still alive in the camps were freed.

Suddenly, people could come out of the shadows. This brought joy. But it also brought sadness. It took time to track everyone down. Many had lost family members. Some children found out they had no family left.

Kloster Indersdorf

After the war, **refugee** centers were set up. Children from all over were brought to them. They came from concentration camps. Others had been in forced labor camps. A few had been in hiding. All wanted to find their families.

The United Nations set up a center for lost children. It was called Kloster Indersdorf.

START OF THE UNITED NATIONS

The United Nations (UN) formed at the end of World War II. Fifty-one nations agreed to work together to promote human rights, peace, and security. Today, nearly every country in the world is part of the UN.

At the center, workers cared for the children. They wanted to make them feel loved. Children ate healthy meals. There were warm beds and hot baths. Doctors gave checkups. Teachers led classes and activities.

Finding children's families was hard. Years had passed. The children looked different. Some did not know their names. They had been too young. Others had been given new names. Many forgot where they were from.

An American photographer visited. He had each child hold up a chalkboard. Their name was written on it. Then he took their picture. Newspapers printed these. The hope was that someone would recognize the children. This happened sometimes. But often no one was left to come get them. These children had to begin new lives.

FAST FACT: Kloster Indersdorf was in a former monastery. Between 1945 and 1948, the center helped more than 1,000 children.

Starting Again

Before the war ended, Nazis tried to empty the concentration camps. They wanted to cover up what they had done. Prisoners were loaded on "death trains." Edith Fox was put on one of these. She rode for three days. There was no food. People lay dying at her feet.

In the night, Edith jumped off the speeding train. The fall broke her nose. Then she hit her head on a tree. But she kept running.

Soon Edith was captured again. She was taken to another camp. They tried to starve her. Four months passed. Then the war ended. Russian troops set her free.

With no family left, Edith didn't want to go home. She wanted to go to America. Edith was staying at a camp for displaced people. After two years, she moved to New York. There, she started a new life.

Edith married and had three children. But she did not talk about her past. It was too painful. She kept her secret for over 70 years.

DISPLACED PERSONS CAMPS

Camps for people displaced by the war were set up in Germany, Austria, and Italy. Between 1945 and 1952, more than 250,000 Jewish people lived in these. Many camps had schools for children. Babies were also born in these camps.

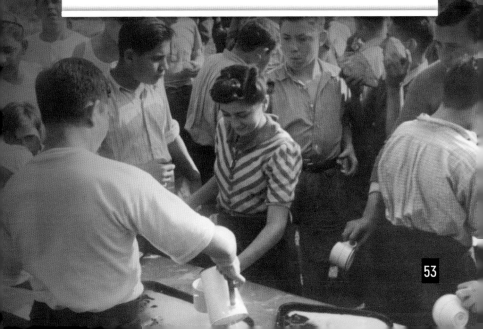

Keeping Traditions Alive

American soldiers came to free prisoners at Buchenwald. There was a pile of dead bodies. Then one soldier saw something move. A young boy was hiding behind the pile. It was Lulek. The soldier took him by the hand. He announced that the war was over.

Naphtali was also at the camp. He had been sent away on a death train. But he jumped off. He returned to find Lulek.

After the war, Naphtali wanted to go to Israel. He said it was the Jewish homeland. The boys would be safe there. They went there on a ship. Many other survivors made the same choice.

Lulek's father had been a **rabbi**. His grandfather and great-grandfather had been too. To honor his family, Lulek followed in their footsteps. He grew up to become Israel's head rabbi.

Speaking Out

Young survivors found homes in new countries. A large number went to the U.S. and Israel. Others went to France or England. Some went as far as Africa or South America.

Many wanted to put the past behind them. They started families and careers. Their stories often stayed hidden. Even family and close friends did not always know.

FAST FACT: By 1952, over 80,000 Jewish people displaced by the war had moved to the United States.

Robert Krell was a child Holocaust survivor. He mostly stayed silent too. It hurt to talk about what he had lost.

Forty years later, he went to a gathering of survivors. The speaker was the head rabbi of Israel, Lulek. Lulek's story made Krell think. He said it was like "a bolt of lightning."

He decided it was time to end his silence. Krell helped start two groups for child Holocaust survivors. Later, he started another program. It taught high school students about the Holocaust.

In a speech, Krell spoke about the importance of remembering. "I am so proud that Holocaust survivors have spoken out," he said. "It is clear that we must remember that which we would rather forget. But we cannot; we are not allowed to forget."

Edith Fox felt the same way. Her story was a secret. Then she turned 90. She decided to share her experience with the local newspaper. "I wanted to tell my story because I'm afraid people are forgetting," she said. "We can never forget what happened. We can never let it happen again."

Glossary

Allied: part of the group of countries that fought against Germany during World War II

anti-Semitic: showing hatred or discrimination against Jewish people

bribe: something valuable given to a person in exchange for better treatment

cellar: a room that is built into the ground; usually used for storage

chancellor: the leader of the government in some European countries

classify: to arrange items or people into groups based on something they have in common

concentration camp: a prison where large groups of people are kept during a war; often they are forced to work and live in very bad conditions

convent: a house or group of buildings where religious workers or students live together

gas chamber: a room where people are killed using poison gas

genocide: the killing of people who belong to an ethnic group

ghetto: a part of a city where Jewish people were forced to live

Holocaust: the murder of millions of Jews, as well as members of other groups, by Nazis during World War II

liberation: the time when countries were freed from Nazi control at the end of World War II

Nazi: a member of a political party that ruled Germany from 1933 to 1945

orphanage: a place where children who don't have parents live and are cared for

rabbi: a Jewish religious leader

refugee: a person who has had to flee a country to escape from war or being attacked

smuggle: to break the law by secretly moving someone or something between countries

synagogue: a Jewish house of worship

underground: secret; not allowed by the government

OLYMPIC GAMES

CHAPTER 2

The Early Games

Ancient Greeks liked sports. They enjoyed competition too. It is no surprise they created the Games. The event let them show off their strength and speed.

Big Differences

The word *Olympics* comes from Olympia. This was a sacred site in Greece. The first Games were held there. It is hard to say when they began. Early writings suggest 776 BC. Experts think it was probably earlier.

These contests were not like those of today. They honored the Greek god Zeus. There were no teams. Each man competed for himself. People loved watching the event. Crowds were small though. Most who went lived nearby.

FAST FACT: There were four years between each Olympics. The ancient Greeks named this period of time. They called it an Olympiad.

CHAPTER 3
A Revival

It was 1890. Nearly 1,500 years had passed. A French man traveled to England. His name was Pierre de Coubertin. While there, he met a man who loved sports. The man was trying to restart the Games. Coubertin was inspired. He wanted to help.

In 1894, Coubertin held a meeting. People came from nine countries. Everyone agreed the event should come back. This was an important meeting. It was the start of the IOC. That stands for International Olympic Committee.

The Games began again in 1896. Athens hosted. Over 240 men from 14 countries took part. They played nine sports. Some raced bikes. Others swam and wrestled. There were 43 events in all. More than 60,000 fans showed up. The revival was a big success.

FAST FACT: The IOC still runs the Games today. It is based in Switzerland. There may be up to 115 members. They are from all over the world.

STRANGE SPORTS

New sports are added to the Olympics each year. Some are also taken away. Club swinging began with the 1904 Games. A man would twirl a club like a baton. He would earn points for his routine. Pigeon shooting was in the 1920 Games. The winner shot 21 live pigeons. About 300 birds were killed in all. People thought it was too bloody. The event lasted just one year. Today, people shoot clay discs instead. Tug-of-war was once an Olympic sport too.

CHAPTER 10
Future Games

The Games face several problems. Cities do not want to lose money. Not all athletes play fair. Safety concerns are also growing. Weather is causing trouble too. Many people are looking for solutions. They want to see the event continue.

No Snow, No Games

Snow is needed for winter sports. But Earth is slowly warming. Experts call this climate change. Some cities get less snow now than in the past. It is only getting worse. Soon they may not be able to hold future Games.

One fix is fake snow. It is made by machines. This is expensive. Large amounts are not easy to make. Fake snow is also lower quality. Natural snow is better.

FAST FACT: Experts have many ideas about how to fight climate change. One is for countries to release fewer greenhouse gases. This could help, but it might not be enough.

WH/TE L/GHTNING BOOKS®
NONFICTION

CHILDREN OF THE HOLOCAUST

9781680217551

CRYPTOCURRENCY

9781680216387

DEADLY BITES

9781680216400

DIGITAL WORLDS

9781680217377

ESPORTS

9781680217391

FLIGHT SQUADS

9781680216912

DROIDS AND ROBOTS

9781680216394

OLYMPIC GAMES

9781680217384

WORKING DOGS

9781680217414

WORLD CUP SOCCER

9781680217407

MORE TITLES COMING SOON
SDLBACK.COM/WHITE-LIGHTNING-BOOKS